A Scr... from the Moon

by Lisa Moore

Harcourt
SCHOOL PUBLISHERS

Printed in China

ISBN 10: 0-15-350566-4
ISBN 13: 978-0-15-350566-9

Ordering Options
ISBN 10: 0-15-350335-1 (Grade 5 Below-Level Collection)
ISBN 13: 978-0-15-350335-1 (Grade 5 Below-Level Collection)
ISBN 10: 0-15-357570-0 (package of 5)
ISBN 13: 978-0-15-357570-9 (package of 5)

5 6 7 8 9 10   468   12 11 10 09

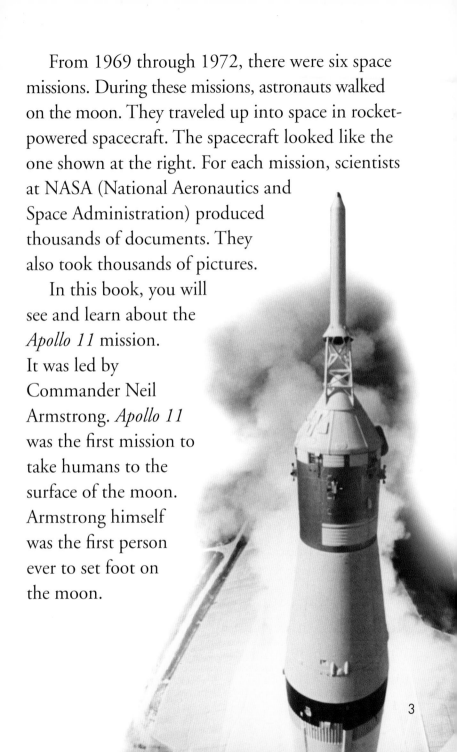

From 1969 through 1972, there were six space missions. During these missions, astronauts walked on the moon. They traveled up into space in rocket-powered spacecraft. The spacecraft looked like the one shown at the right. For each mission, scientists at NASA (National Aeronautics and Space Administration) produced thousands of documents. They also took thousands of pictures.

In this book, you will see and learn about the *Apollo 11* mission. It was led by Commander Neil Armstrong. *Apollo 11* was the first mission to take humans to the surface of the moon. Armstrong himself was the first person ever to set foot on the moon.

3

When Armstrong was growing up, he probably never guessed that one day he would walk on the moon. His aspirations were, literally, not quite so lofty. Armstrong dreamed of being a pilot. He made a wind tunnel in his basement. He used it to test model airplanes. When he was old enough, he worked several after-school jobs so he could afford to get his pilot's license. He finally got his pilot's license when he was only sixteen. This was before he even got his driver's license!

Armstrong later went to Purdue University in Indiana on a scholarship from the United States Navy. He left Purdue to serve with the navy in Korea in 1950. When he returned, he finished his degree in aeronautical engineering. After that, he began working at NASA as a pilot. In 1962, he was given astronaut status. This meant that he could join missions that would take him into space. He trained very hard for several years and flew many important missions.

Finally, in 1969, Armstrong got the chance of a lifetime: to be the commander of the *Apollo 11* mission. Below is a picture of the crew of *Apollo 11*. That's Neil Armstrong on the left. Next is Michael Collins, the pilot of the command module. It carried the astronauts from earth to the moon's orbit. On the right is Buzz Aldrin, the pilot of the lunar module. The lunar module took Aldrin and Armstrong to the surface of the moon.

These three astronauts were the only people to really travel to the moon during the *Apollo 11* mission. However, hundreds of other people were in charge of getting them there and back safely. NASA staff managed training. They also monitored every part of the mission from the ground. In addition, members of a backup crew had to be ready at all times before the launch. This was in case one or more of the *Apollo 11* crew got sick or hurt and could not go to the moon.

This photograph froze the moment the *Saturn V* rocket ignited on July 16, 1969. If you had been there, you would have been squinting from the glare. This photograph lets you look directly at it.

Between 1964 and 1973, the United States spent $6.5 billion on *Saturn V* rockets. NASA launched thirteen of them from 1967 to 1973. The rockets towered 364 feet (111 m) and were 33 feet (10 m) around. Each one weighed 6.5 million pounds (2.9 million kg). On top of each rocket was the module that held the astronauts. About the size of a car, it was a little cramped for three people.

After the rocket did its job, the huge rocket parts were jettisoned, or dropped, in space. The module went on without the rocket. After many years of developing such complex structures, NASA needed most of that rocket for only about twenty minutes of work!

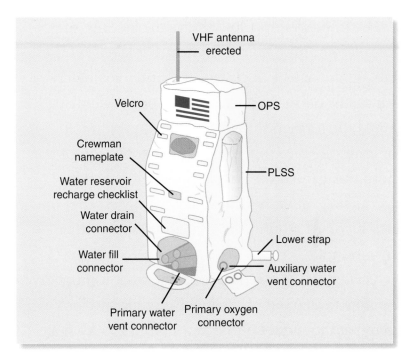

VHF antenna erected

Velcro

OPS

Crewman nameplate

PLSS

Water reservoir recharge checklist

Water drain connector

Lower strap

Water fill connector

Auxiliary water vent connector

Primary water vent connector

Primary oxygen connector

On the moon, the astronauts wore big white space suits. They also carried big white backpacks. This is a drawing of the backpack. On the bottom was the Personal Life Support System (PLSS). On the top was the Oxygen Purge System (OPS). The insides of both were full of hoses, batteries, and tanks. The VHF antenna on the top let astronauts talk clearly with each other and with Mission Control back in Houston, Texas. It was important that their voices not be muffled. This backpack was the most important thing an astronaut had to survive.

The photograph below shows the landing sites of *Apollo 11* and *Apollo 12*. The other labels on the map are the names of craters and other geological formations on the surface of the moon. Scientists named the formations after people they admired. For example, the Copernicus crater at the top of the photo was named for Nicolaus Copernicus. He was the first modern astronomer to suggest that the earth revolved around the sun, and not the other way around.

As you look at this map, imagine what it must have been like to step out of the lunar module and look around at the surface of the moon. It has rocky ridges and craters. Astronaut Buzz Aldrin described this amazing and eerily tranquil view as "magnificent desolation."

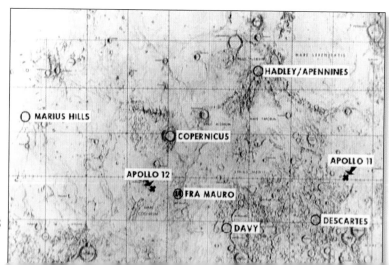

Of course, the astronauts' trips to the moon were not all sight-seeing. They had to study the moon as scientists. They had to operate very complicated equipment! One mistake could potentially put the mission and the astronauts in danger. Because of this, everything the astronauts had to do was written in checklists. The checklists made sure that everything—from testing the life support systems in the lunar module, to jettisoning rocket stages, to putting cameras away after they were used—would be remembered.

This photograph was taken during training for the flight. It shows two of the *Apollo 11* astronauts practicing using the equipment. It is the same equipment they would be using on the moon. One astronaut appears to be using a tool for grabbing chunks of rock from the surface of the moon. The six Apollo missions brought back 842 pounds (382 kg) of rocks, sand, and dust from the moon. Today these moon rocks are kept in the Lunar Sample Building at the Johnson Space Center in Houston. Almost 1,000 samples are loaned to schools and scientists each year.

The practice that the astronauts got during training sessions paid off when they finally reached the moon. They were now used to carrying out their experiments while wearing space suits and big, heavy backpacks. In this photograph, Buzz Aldrin is carrying out an experiment to figure out the contents of "solar wind." Solar wind includes the electrically charged particles released by the sun.

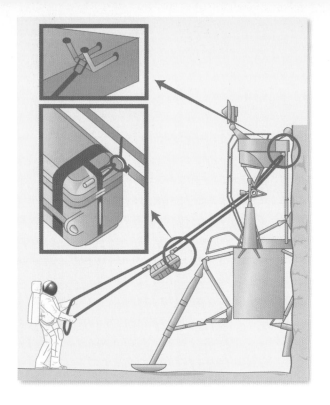

This diagram showed something called the Lunar Equipment Conveyor. It let an astronaut move something back into the Lunar Module.

This page was part of a long document called Lunar Structures Handout. It had sixty pages of drawings of all kinds of things. They included antennas, doors, hammers, landing gear, shields, and vents. Many drawings showed astronauts how to set up and use the equipment they had onboard.

This photograph of the earth was taken from the Command Module, *Columbia,* on July 20, 1969. That was the day the astronauts first walked on the moon. You can see Australia on the left. It's just above the horizon.

This is not a real photograph. Twelve astronauts never stood on the moon at once. Bob Farwell made this collage in 2001. It must have been fun.

Hopefully, these images from the "Apollo Lunar Surface Journal" will inspire you. Maybe one day you, too, will visit a world beyond your own. If you do, keep all of your drawings. You should also take a lot of photographs. Then you can make a scrapbook, too.

Think Critically

1. Why was the astronaut backpack important?

2. Write three sentences from this book that state a fact and three that state an opinion.

3. Can you classify the images in this book into two or three types? What would they be?

4. Which image in this book did you find the most interesting? Why did you choose this one?

5. What do these pictures and diagrams help the reader understand about being an astronaut?

 **Science**

More About the Moon Do research on the Internet or use other library resources to learn more about the moon. Make a poster of your findings.

School-Home Connection Ask older family members or friends where they were when the *Apollo 11* astronauts first walked on the moon. Discuss what they remember of that historical event.

Word Count: 1,248 (with graphics 1,290)